Endangered Animals
of the
RAIN FOREST

By
Sandra Uchitel

Illustrated by
Serge Michaels

PRICE STERN SLOAN

Los Angeles

To my Son, to the Hedgehog and the Vole,
to past and present friends whose **VISIONS**,
both great and small, we now recall. . . .

ABOUT THE AUTHOR AND THE ILLUSTRATOR

Sandra Uchitel *is an archaeologist who has traveled extensively in Africa, Central and South America in the role of wildlife photographer, journalist and on archaeological research projects. In the Amazon region of Brazil, she saw endangered animals caged for shipment, to be sold illegally. She also saw piles of skins from jaguars, ocelots and snakes, tanned and ready to be sent to various countries for fur coats, shoes and handbags. While on safari in Africa, she witnessed the beauty of nature represented by thousands of migrating herds on the Serengeti Plains, but also the skeletal remains of elephants and rhinos without their ivory tusks and horns. Sandra has written this book to help educate the children of the world.*

Serge Michaels *has been drawing ever since he can remember. His earliest illustrations were crayon renderings on the family living room walls. When he grew up, he attended Pratt Institute in New York City and the Skowhegan School in Maine. This led to his being selected by Walt Disney Studios for their Feature Animation Division, where he worked on such films as* Little Mermaid, The Rescuers Down Under, *and* Beauty and the Beast. *Serge enjoys painting and drawing from life. For this book he made frequent trips to the zoo to try to get inside the character of each animal. He will continue his animal studies when he travels to Africa to work on his next project. He credits Jerry Pinkney, the highly respected children's book artist, for being a great inspirational mentor in his career.*

*A special thanks to Shambala Preserve for their generosity and
for helping to love and care for all God's creatures.*

Library of Congress Cataloging-in-Publication Data

Uchitel, Sandra.
    Endangered animals of the rain forests/by Sandra Uchitel;
    illustrations by Serge Michaels.
          p.   cm.
    Summary: Describes the characteristics of tropical rain forests, examines the plight of its endangered animals, and discusses how readers can help save these threatened areas.
    ISBN 0-8431-2994-8
    1. Endangered species—Juvenile literature. 2. Endangered species—Tropics—Juvenile literature. 3. Rain forest fauna—Juvenile literature. 4. Rain forest ecology—Juvenile literature. 5. Wildlife conservation—Juvenile literature. [1. Rain forest animals. 2. Rare animals. 3. Rain forests. 4. Wildlife conservation.]
    I. Michaels, Serge, ill. II. Title.
    QL83.U24   1992
    591.52'9'0913—dc20
                                    91-28591
                                    CIP
                                    AC

This book has been printed on recycled paper.

To the Children of the World

We will never view our Earth the way it used to look;
Far too many pages have been torn from nature's book.

Now's the time for us to care. With your help we can reverse
The damage we've inflicted upon our universe.

Jungle forests, tall and deep, are where the creatures fly and creep.
We must keep them alive; without our love they'll not survive.

And someday when your children ask, "Did you do your part?"
You can look into their eyes and say, "I tried with all my heart."

From the beautiful and noble to the ugly and maligned,
They deserve our help—they're nature's gift to humankind.

What Is a Rain Forest?

Tropical rain forests have existed for millions of years, and most of them are located in a broad, green belt around the equator. Some small areas fall outside this region, such as the east coast of Australia and the Atlantic Forest on the Brazilian coast. Tropical rain forests do not have changing seasons; their year-round temperature is between 75 and 80 degrees Fahrenheit. True rain forests receive over thirty-three feet of rain a year.

Only seven percent of the Earth's surface is covered by rain forests. However, approximately 65 percent of our Earth's plant and animal species live in these regions. In Costa Rica's tropical forests alone, it is estimated that 850 species of bird, 700 species of butterfly and 200 species of mammal are present. Untold numbers of plants and animals are waiting to be discovered in these tropical centers of vital natural resources.

Some of the most important areas of tropical rain forest exist in Central and South America, with Brazil containing the world's largest. Others can be found in the mountains of Africa and Southeast Asia.

Rain forests are made up of four layers: the Forest Floor; the Understory or Lower Canopy; the Upper Canopy; and the Emergent Layer or Sunlit Zone. Each layer differs greatly in the amount of sunlight, air and wind it receives. The temperature within each layer also varies, therefore climate dictates the types of plants and animals that live in, or visit, the different layers.

FOREST FLOOR

The Forest Floor is very dark. Only about 2 percent of the sun's light reaches there, so green plan[ts] cannot grow. Only fungi that live on decaying leaves and trees survive on the ground floor. The humidity [is] very high (95 to 100 percent), and the temperature is usually 75 degrees F. The air is still. Because it is [so] humid, the Forest Floor is always damp and soggy. Although this would be unpleasant for most peop[le], many animals, insects and reptiles thrive on its plentiful supply of food. Ants by the millions, along w[ith] crabs, beetles and worms, swarm over rotting vegetation. Predators, and those preyed upon, ha[ve] developed remarkable skin colorings for camouflage, as well as other methods of defense. The Malay[an] tapir's black-and-white coat helps him blend into this darkness, as does the anaconda's mottled skin a[nd] the ocelot's and jaguar's spots, while the armadillo has armor to protect him.

UNDERSTORY OR LOWER CANOPY

The Understory, or Lower Canopy, receives only a small amount of light and rain because of the Upp[er] Canopy's giant umbrella of leaves. Here the climate is milder than it is on the Forest Floor, winds a[re] reduced, but the humidity is still high. At this level, there is great competition for light and water, limiting t[he] types of vegetation found here. The trees grow only 12 to 20 feet tall. In some cases, certain species [of] trees don't get a chance to grow until one of the older trees in the Upper Canopy falls and creates a hole [of] light in the umbrella above. Because of the Understory's dim light, flowers growing on the tree trunks a[nd] branches are very brightly colored. Their brilliance attracts insects that pollinate the flowers, allowing them [to] reproduce. Many different butterflies, frogs, ants and bees live and forage for food in the Understory. Gorill[as] build nests in the trees, while pythons, leopards and vipers lurk in the tangled vines and tree branches.

1. **South American Jaguar**
2. **Three-Toed Sloth**
3. **Dumeril's Ground Boa**
4. **Mountain Gorilla**
5. **Ocelot**
6. **Giant River Otter**

120 feet

Emergent Layer or
Sunlit Zone

90 feet

Upper Canopy

60 feet

②

④

Understory or
Lower Canopy

30 feet

Forest Floor

③

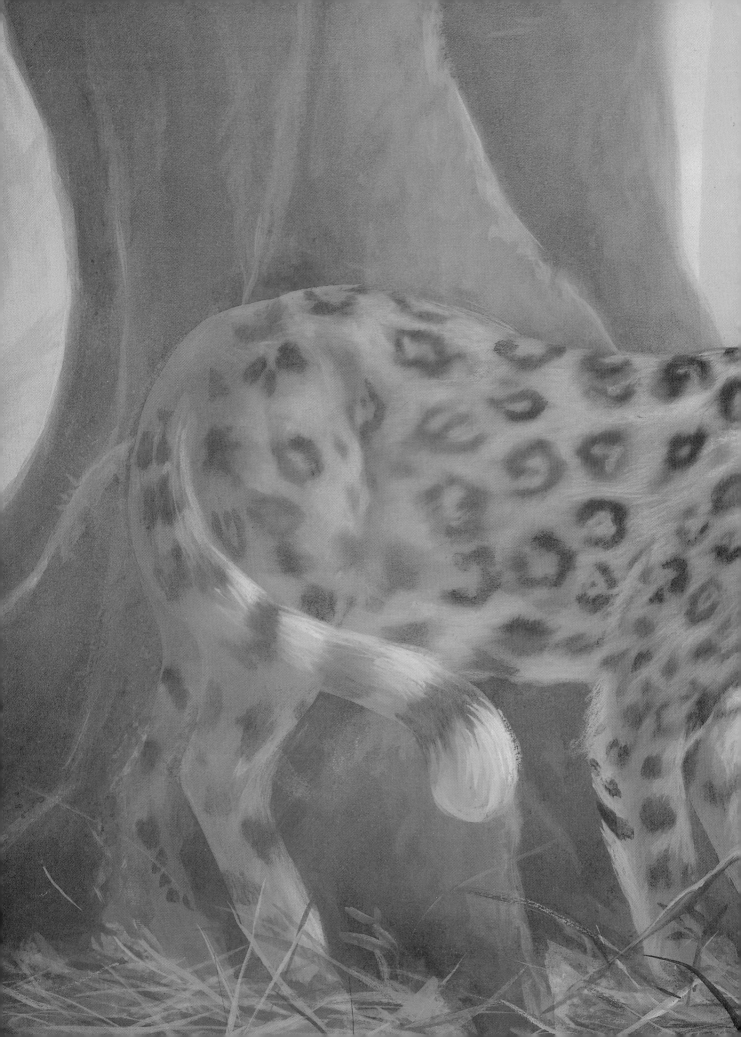

SOUTH AMERICAN JAGUAR

The jungle nights
are dark and deep
Where we prowl
on padded feet.

Our fur is gorgeous,
people say,
That's why they take
our lives away.

The Jaguar's last stronghold is the Amazon Basin Region of Brazil and Guatemala's rain-drenched cloud forests. Rain forests are being destroyed at an alarming rate (in Brazil, 150 acres every minute) by farmers seeking land, by miners hunting for gold and by paper companies needing trees. As well as losing their homeland, Jaguars have been hunted for their skins and captured for illegal export. Brazilian and Guatemalan rain forests are critical to their survival in the wild.

ENDANGERED
The South American Jaguar

CRITICALLY ENDANGERED
The Mexican Jaguar is near extinction.

EXTINCT
Arizona Jaguar, circa 1905

THREE-TOED SLOTH

I'm a simple, slow
and sluggish sloth.
My toes grasp trees
to stay aloft.

To jungle friends,
I'm not a stranger;
As forests shrink,
I face grave danger.

Two-toed and Three-toed Sloths are found in the flooded parts of Central and South American forests. Sloths spend most of their lives hanging upside down by their long claws on each foot. Nothing can dislodge them from their perch. Adult Sloths have a greenish cast caused by algae growing on their fur. This helps Sloths remain undetected. Baby Sloths do not have this green algae until several months after birth. These slow-moving creatures live only in rain forests so if the forests disappear, then so do the Sloths.

ENDANGERED
Two-Toed and Three-Toed Sloth

DUMERIL'S GROUND BOA

I coil myself
in leaves and trees,
And catch my dinner
with one big squeeze.

Don't buy belts or shoes
made from my hide.
For these possessions,
my friends have died.

Boas are nonpoisonous and kill by constriction. Dumeril's Ground Boa is found in the humid rain forests of Madagascar and the Mascarene Islands. This snake has been killed for its beautiful skin, and captured and sold as a pet. It is not dangerous to humans. Every creature has its place in the wild, and by destroying one group, the balance of nature is disrupted.

ENDANGERED

Dumeril's Ground Boa, Anaconda, Jamaican Boa, Puerto Rican Boa

CRITICALLY ENDANGERED

Kell-Scaled Boa (only seven left)

EXTINCT

With only one to three left, the Round Island Boa, circa 1974, is, in effect, extinct.

MOUNTAIN GORILLA

While some think I'm scary,
I'm really quite mellow,
Even though I beat my chest
as I roar and bellow.

Man has killed my friends
to make ashtrays from their hands.
Now my whole forest home
is what he demands.

The Mountain Gorilla is the largest of the two subspecies, the Mountain and the Lowland Gorilla. Mountain Gorillas live in the rain forests of Africa, and are in danger of losing their forest home as people's need for land continues to grow. The gorilla is not a meat-eater, but lives only on fruit and vegetables.

CRITICALLY ENDANGERED

Fewer than 500 Mountain and Lowland Gorillas combined survive in the wild.

OCELOT

Man built on the deserts
where I used to roam,
So now it's the jungle
I call home.

My spotted skin
caught people's fancy;
Destroying my habitat
leaves my life chancy.

Also known as the Painted Leopard, the Ocelot is a medium-size wildcat that formerly lived in the Southwestern United States and Mexico. Few, if any, remain there today. The Ocelot now ranges in the dense forests of Central and South America. They have been killed for their skins (to make coats, handbags and hats) and illegally exported as pets. Although the Ocelot is harmless to humans, and will even run away from a dog, it does not make a good pet. Wild animals belong in the wild.

ENDANGERED
Central and South American Ocelot

GIANT RIVER OTTER

My feet are webbed,
my soles are hairy,
Jungle rivers are
my sanctuary.

When man destroys
the water and land,
We lose our lives—
not nature's plan.

Once hunted for their valuable fur, Giant River Otters are slowly making a comeback. However, as the rain forests are cleared and towns are built, pollution from logging and human habitation threatens all river life.

ENDANGERED
The Giant River Otter

120 feet

Emergent Layer or Sunlit Zone

90 feet

Upper Canopy

60 feet

Understory or Lower Canopy

30 feet

Forest Floor

UPPER CANOPY

The Upper Canopy spreads its matted covering 75 to 90 feet above the Forest Floor. The leaves and branches of the trees overlap and weave, forming a dense maze of vegetation. Vines called "lianas" climb up the trees, then reach out, connecting one tree to the next to form the netting that ties the canopy together. This umbrella absorbs more than 98 percent of all sunlight. The leaves of the trees in this layer adapt to the large amount of light and rain by having smooth surfaces, pointed tips and a large vein that acts as a gutter for rainfall. Orchids, ferns and other plants, along with nearly half the rain forest mammals, live in this area with its abundance of light and food. Parrots, Quetzal birds, Red Colobus and Howler Monkeys, Slow Loris, flying squirrels, insects and butterflies are among the many creatures that make their homes in the Upper Canopy.

EMERGENT LAYER OR SUNLIT ZONE

This is the uppermost level of the rain forest, where the tops of the oldest trees, some as tall as 90 and 150 feet, are bathed in sunlight. Since only a few of the oldest trees reach such great heights, the vegetation of the Sunlit Zone is not dense. At this level, treetops are exposed to the highest winds, brightest sun, lowest humidity and most radical temperature changes. To adapt to the high winds, bright light and extremes in temperature, the leaves of the trees are smaller and waxier. In fact, at this level, when the sun is its hottest, the plants actually sleep and photosynthesis stops. Parrots, Harpy Eagles, certain monkeys, insects and reptiles visit and live in this layer.

The world's tropical rain forests have four major threats to their existence: logging; farmers clearing and burning vast areas to plant crops; cattle ranching; and illegal wildlife trading. More than 20 million acres of rain forests are converted each year for farming, and more than 10 million acres are destroyed yearly by logging. If these practices continue, by the year 2000 the Earth's rain forests will disappear. The rain forest animals, butterflies, trees, frogs, orchids, ferns and countless undiscovered species and cures for illnesses will all be gone.

7. Galago (Bush Baby)
8. Harpy Eagle
9. Spix's Macaw
10. Red Howler Monkey
11. Resplendent Quetzal
12. Golden Lion Tamarin

GALAGO

I'm a playful, agile,
tree-bound creature.
Bush Baby's my nickname;
nature's my teacher.

When the forests are gone,
people must take the blame.
If the trees disappear,
then we'll do the same.

Found in the equatorial rain forests of Africa, the Galago (or Bush Baby) is a small, nocturnal primate with soft, thick fur and long hind legs. Because of its legs, the Bush Baby can leap with great agility. It also has a strange habit of licking the palms of its hands and the soles of its feet as it climbs among the trees. Another name for it is the Night Ape. Pictured is the Dwarf Galago, the smallest of all, about the size of a rat.

ENDANGERED
Galago

HARPY EAGLE

I fly above the forest,
with the sharp eyes of an eagle.
My crown of plumage makes
me elegant and regal.

The rain forest's my home,
but as trees are chopped down,
I lose my high perch,
and man builds another town.

The Harpy is the largest and most powerful eagle. He can be seen soaring above the forest canopies in Brazil and Guatemala. Loss of jungle habitat will severely threaten this majestic bird.

ENDANGERED

Harpy Eagle of South America, Bald Eagle, Golden Eagle,
Monkey-Eating Eagle, Crested Eagle, Imperial Eagle

EXTINCT

Madagascar Serpent Eagle, circa 1950

SPIX'S MACAW

A coat of many colors
is my best feature.
I waken the jungle;
I'm a noisy screecher.

Killing for feathers
was long ago banned,
But now they're taking
my trees and my land.

Nearly 340 species of parrot exist in the world, and most are rain forest dwellers. Spix's Macaws live in the Brazilian rain forest. Land clearing and logging of the forest destroys their natural habitat. Among other things, their beautiful feathers have been used for hats and costume decoration. Many species of the parrot are still sold as pets.

ENDANGERED
*Amazon Parrot, Hanging Parrot, Red-Necked Parrot, Cayman Brac Parrot,
Indigo-Winged Parrot, Guayaquil Great Green Macaw*

CRITICALLY ENDANGERED
Spix's Macaw of Brazil

EXTINCT
*Rodriquez Parrot, circa 1800; Mascarene Parrot,
circa 1840; Cuban Red Macaw, circa 1864*

RED HOWLER MONKEY

My grasping tail
is like an extra arm,
As I leap between trees
and sound my alarm.

Logging our forest
destroys trees as tall as giants,
and kills plants and animals
still unknown to science.

Red Howler Monkeys inhabit tropical America. The striking feature of Howler Monkeys is their voice, which can be heard for miles. Destruction of the forests now threatens their existence in the wild.

ENDANGERED

*Howler Monkey, Black Spider Monkey, Central American Squirrel Monkey,
Long-Haired Spider Monkey, Proboscis Monkey*

CRITICALLY ENDANGERED

The Yellow-Tailed Woolly Monkey of the Peruvian Andes

RESPLENDENT QUETZAL

According to legend,
I'm a bird of liberty
Requiring freedom,
not captivity.

If you let the rain forests
all disappear,
You'll be killing the Earth
and its atmosphere.

The striking emerald green Quetzal is nearly four feet long, and is found in the forests of Central and South America. This bird, which is the national emblem of Guatemala, is pictured on that country's currency. The Quetzal eats insects, berries, tree frogs and snails.

ENDANGERED
Resplendent Quetzal

GOLDEN LION TAMARIN

Before people saved me
from my terrible plight,
My song would've been missed
from the jungle at night.

But a new chance came
with captive breeding;
It's what many endangered species
are needing.

Golden Lion Tamarins were almost extinct until captive-breeding programs reintroduced them to their natural habitat on protective preserves in their native Brazilian forests. Without the help of people, this beautiful animal was doomed, as are so many other creatures of our rain forests. The Golden Lion Tamarin weighs only 21 ounces and eats insects. Another Tamarin species, the Black-Faced Lion Tamarin, was just discovered in 1990. It is important to protect our rain forests because, even today, we do not know all the creatures that live there.

CRITICALLY ENDANGERED
Golden Lion Tamarin and the Black-Faced Lion Tamarin

How You Can Help Save the Rain Forests and the Animals That Live There

You might think, "Hey, I'm just a kid—I can't help until I'm older." **Wrong.** Each and every thing you do to help save our world and the animals that live in it will make a big difference.

1. **Separate your garbage.** If we separate paper, plastic containers, glass and aluminum, we can use them again. We are running out of places to dump our garbage—let's reuse everything we can.

   Paper: Save all paper—newspapers, junk mail, old school tests and cardboard boxes. Get your teachers to save all paper from your school, then take it to your local recycling center. If every person in the United States recycled his or her newspapers, 500,000 trees would be saved each year. Think of all the trees we could save if the entire world recycled newspapers.

   Cans: All the soda pop that you and your friends drink could be earning you money. Save all cans and turn them in. Once you start saving, you'll be surprised at how much you can earn.

   Glass and Plastic: Save all bottles and jars. Put them in a separate box for recycling and redeem them.

   Once you start saving and recycling everything, the next step is to organize your friends and neighbors to do the same. Form a recycling club in your area. Collect paper, plastic bottles, cans and glass from all your neighbors who don't have time to do it themselves. Ring their doorbell and ask if they will help save our rain forests.

2. **Learn more about our endangered rain forests.** Ask your teachers, go to the library or your local museum. Get involved.

3. **Visit zoos, parks and woodlands.** These visits will help you to see and understand the wonders of nature. If you have a backyard, encourage wildlife to live there. If you don't have a backyard, you can put up a bird feeder, or plant a tree on the street in front of your house. Go to your local parks and clean them up.

4. **Write letters to the congressman and senator of your state.** Don't be shy. Write the President and tell him how much you care about our world.

5. **Try to get your parents to assist you.** The animals of our world need their help too.

6. **Try not to eat anything served in a Styrofoam container.** Ask to have it put in paper. Don't be embarrassed and don't give up. If enough people refuse to eat things served in Styrofoam, large companies will get the message. They don't want to lose money, so they will start serving everything wrapped in recycled paper. Your recycled newspaper will eventually become a wrapper for a cheeseburger. Styrofoam is a destroyer of our precious ozone, and it is not biodegradable.

7. **Never buy animals that belong in the wild.** Wild animals do not make good pets.

8. **Eat only canned tuna that is DOLPHIN SAFE.** Many fishing boats use nets that do not allow dolphins to escape. Many dolphins die tangled and strangled in tuna fishing nets. If we eat only dolphin-safe tuna, we are saving thousands of dolphins yearly.

9. **Do not buy any product that is made by killing an endangered animal.** This means animal skins, hats with eagle feathers, turtleshell combs or souvenirs, snakeskin shoes or handbags and ivory products.

10. **Think of the world and how you can help make a difference.**